ABOUT THIS BOOK . . .

For the past twelve years, Joe Bayly has taught a Sunday school class of adults. "Actually," he explains, "over the years it has evolved into a transgenerational class: grandparents, parents and their college-age children. At times high-school ones, too. And singles, including the unmarried, divorced and widowed. It's an exciting mix." He has also taught high-school and young-adult classes.

Out of his experience as a teacher, and with the added background of his contacts with thousands of other teachers in churches and in Sunday school conventions across the United States and Canada, Joe Bayly has written these ideas about teaching, in the form of a diary. They range from the joy of teaching to how to handle the person who always has something to say, and the one who expresses doubt. "I failed today" will strike a responsive chord in most teachers who read this little book.

While the "diary" covers a year, incidents and experiences included represent a number of teaching years, collapsed in time. These same incidents, the author says, "represent real people. In most cases I've tried to conceal their identity. If the concealment is inadequate in places, I'm sorry."

These ideas are not just for those who teach teens and adults. Most of them are universal, applicable to those who teach younger ages as well.

D0684273

I LOVE TO TELL THE STORY

Joseph Bayly

David C. Cook Publishing Co.

ELGIN, ILLINOIS—WESTON, ONTARIO
FULLERTON, CALIFORNIA

I LOVE TO TELL THE STORY
Copyright © 1978 David C. Cook Publishing Co.

Published by David C. Cook Publishing Co., Elgin, IL 60120
Edited by Linda Girard
Designed by Kurt Dietsch

Printed in the United States of America
Library of Congress Catalog Number: 78-61299
ISBN: 0-89191-162-6

First Printing: September 1978
Second Printing: April 1980

To Covenant Class
and to Ken
with whom I've shared
the joy of teaching
during these years
and to Kenny
who has taught us all
the joy of simple faith and love

CONTENTS

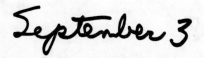

September 3

It's fun to teach.

I know it's a heavy responsibility, it takes time for preparation, it ties me down, it's draining, it's hard to get through the lessons when I have a headache—but it's fun.

To see comprehension replace puzzlement on a student's face, to hear words of certainty from one who not long ago was filled with doubt, to follow another into the joy of discovery, share a smile or laugh, be aware of quiet trust and expectant waiting, feel warmth and respect and love—it's fun to teach.

It's awesome to teach.

To speak for God, to explain His Word, point out the way, share with others the lessons His Spirit is teaching me—it's awesome to teach.

I teach with fear and trembling, fear lest I obscure the way rather than reveal its radiant track, trembling lest I be a hypocrite, castaway.

Yet I teach. With faith in God, by faith in God, I teach . . . the God, "who is able to keep you from falling, and to present you faultless before the presence of His glory with exceeding joy . . ."

And teaching, I am taught. My teachers are God and my class. Each teaches me of the other, each brings me closer to the other.

Tomorrow is the beginning of a new teaching period, the fall quarter. Vacations are over; children have returned to school; the church program is back to normal.

September 8

Yesterday I was reading about England in 1780, when the first Sunday school was organized.

England had just lost an unpopular war with the small American colonies. A spirit of revolution was in the air. France's devastating revolution was only nine years in the future.

Children in England were being exploited as a cheap source of labor. Boys and girls as young as seven and eight were forced to work 50 to 60 hours a week—every day except Sunday—in mines, sweatshops and factories.

At this low point in British history a publisher, Robert Raikes of Gloucester, started the first Sunday school. He seems to have gotten the idea for such a school from the wife of Samuel Bradburn, one of John Wesley's most noted preachers.

"Raikes' Ragged School" was what people, including many church people, jeeringly called it, when the publisher gathered children from the lower classes on Sunday afternoons to teach them how to read and write.

The Bible was his textbook. As a result, those poor exploited children were not merely freed from the bondage of illiteracy; they were also freed from the bondage of sin. As the prototypes of tens of millions during the next two hundred years, those children discovered in Sunday school the glorious freedom of becoming sons and daughters of God.

Nobody in 1780 could have foreseen the long-range effects of that Christian act of Robert Raikes: to teach children on Sunday afternoon. Raikes simply did it as his Christian duty.

Historians tell us that the Wesleyan Revival and the Sunday school, which spread from Gloucester throughout the British Isles, kept England from a disastrous revolution such as the French experienced.

The thing that impresses me—especially today, when so many people are saying Sunday school is on its way out because of the critical, godless days we're living in—is that Sunday school was born in crisis and has been strongest in times of crisis . . . for 200 years.

Who knows what the effects of the Sunday school in our church may be? After all, God is the same in the United States and Canada today as He was in England in 1780.

September 12

What kind of teacher do I want to be? How would I describe myself if I were writing a letter to the class during a period of prolonged absence?

Those questions occurred to me when I read I Thessalonians 2:4-13 this morning, because St. Paul wrote about that very matter in this passage.

"I didn't flatter you; I didn't covet anything from you, I didn't look for praise or glory from you," the apostle said.

"Instead, I treated you gently, as a nursing mother treats her child. I comforted you and commanded you, as a father does his children.

"I was filled with affection for you, willing to share not only the gospel with you, but my very life. This was because you were dear to me."

Gentle as a nursing mother, dependable and comforting as a father, filled with feelings of affection, sharing the Word of God—but also my very life . . . *God, make me that sort of teacher.*

September 22

I think one difference between teaching a Sunday school class today and the teaching Jesus did is that Jesus usually taught out-of-doors, where there was always something to tie his lessons to.

I teach in a bare room. (Idea: Next Sunday, be sure to take the Hook teaching picture of Jesus' conversation with Nicodemus, and tape it up on the wall, since we'll be studying that chapter.)

What I mean is, Jesus could say, "The fields are ready to be harvested," because He was walking through them with His class. Or "Behold the birds of the air," or "the lilies of the field," because the members of His class could see them or smell them.

I can't do that. I wish I could. Maybe Sunday school should be held in the park, when the weather's good enough.

But wait a minute. I think there's something more important about Jesus' teaching than having the whole outdoors for His illustrations.

He started His lesson with where people were. He wasn't in the marketplace when He spoke about the poor woman counting her money to see if she had enough to take two sparrows home for supper or not. He wasn't at the tower that fell and killed people when He used that incident to raise the question of evil and God's judgment.

But he was talking to people who knew about poverty and catastrophe. So he began his lesson where the people were, the people He was teaching.

And I can, too. I don't need the out-of-doors; I do need to understand the hopes and fears, joys and sorrows, doubts and perplexities of my class.

October 5

Why do I teach Sunday school? The question sometimes comes to me.

Because they needed a teacher; because someone asked me to; because I like people; because teaching forces me to study the Bible; because I want to help influence the next generation for God; because I have at least a small gift for getting through to adults—helping them think and discuss—and I feel responsible to use it.

All good reasons, I guess. But not the key one, the best one perhaps—the one that will hold me when all else fails.

I teach because the last words Jesus spoke before He ascended to heaven were these: "Go ye therefore and teach . . ." (Matthew 28:19) I teach my Sunday school class because Jesus commanded His followers—and I believe that includes me—to teach His Word.

During this century, we've put a lot of emphasis on the word "Go"—this is a strong basis for foreign missions. But the real emphasis in this verse is on "Teach": "While you are going, teach."

My pattern of life is to teach others, especially my Sunday school class, the things Jesus teaches me.

October 16

I've been reading about the Early Church in the Book of Acts. (Doesn't it seem as if it should be "The Acts of the Holy Spirit" instead of "The Acts of the Apostles"? No, I guess it should be both, since the Spirit works through men.)

This reading in Acts has impressed me with some similarities between my Sunday school class and the Early Church. The Early Church met regularly: so does my class. The Early Church met around the Word, the Bible was central: it's central in my class, too. Jesus promised to be in their midst, even if they only numbered two or three: we've never gotten that few in number, although we approached it several years ago, the Sunday of the big snowstorm. And the men and women in the Early Church had fellowship with each other, they cared for each other: so do the members of my class.

It's easier to share needs in the smaller, less formal room where our class meets than it is in the church worship service. The smaller size of group helps, too.

In a way, we're a church within a church.

Since this is so, I have to be careful as the teacher that we never discuss the affairs of the church itself, that we never criticize the leadership, that we always are loving toward those who are not in the class.

I want the pastor to know that he can count on us to stand with him in building a strong church, for God's glory.

October 26

I was going through some old papers last night, and came upon these pages of lined paper, in my great-grandmother's handwriting. I've often read them, to remind me of my Christian heritage.

During the War Between the States, my great-grandparents lived on a farm outside Gettysburg, Pennsylvania. Their fields were part of the tragic battlefield, their barn was taken over and used as a hospital.

"On Sunday afternoon" great-grandmother Bayly wrote, "as was our custom, my husband Joseph and I walked to the schoolhouse to hold Sunday school. However, the noise of troop movements and cannon in the distance was so great that we could not hold the children's attention. Therefore we dismissed the school early."

Another crisis in our history, another time when Sunday school helped preserve stability and spiritual values.

—I'm glad my great-grandparents were involved in teaching Sunday school. And I'm glad they had the commonsense not to try to compete with a war. (Some teachers I know would say, "Battle or no battle, you remain in your seats until the hour is over.")

November 4

I have to be a Christian person if I'm to teach others how to be Christian persons. I have to know Jesus Christ by faith if I'm to teach others how to know Him.

Otherwise, in those words of Charles Haddon Spurgeon, the nineteenth century Bible teacher, I'm "a blind man elevated to the chair of optics in a university, a deaf man appointed to lead a symphony orchestra, a toad trying to teach eaglets to fly."

The place where I have to begin as a teacher is to be sure that I know "the old, old story of Jesus and His love."

"For God so loved the world, that He gave His only begotten Son, that whosoever believeth in Him should not perish, but have everlasting life." (John 3:16)

I believe those words, that promise. So I can share my faith—small though it is—with my class tomorrow morning.

November 13

I spoke at a Sunday school convention in New Hampshire last week.

During a workshop, I asked the people if there was one Sunday school teacher from their own childhood they remembered above the rest. About half of them answered yes, there was. So I asked why, and they had some interesting answers—like the ones I've had in other places.

"I was special to her. I could tell she was pleased that I was in the class."

"He came over to the schoolyard during the week to play ball with us."

"She told me my dress was pretty. We were poor, and my own mother and father were so busy they probably didn't have time to notice me or compliment me. But my Sunday school teacher did."

One woman said, "My mother died when I was eight years old. My Sunday school teacher literally carried me through the next two years by her love for me."

What always strikes me when I ask that question, "Why was the teacher special?" is how it's the caring that people remember, the love, the affirmation those teachers gave to their students by their words and actions.

I'm pretty sure they must have known the Bible, must have prepared carefully. But that's not what these grown-up men and women remember years later . . . when they have picked up the responsibility for teaching and caring.

A Sunday school teacher doesn't just teach the lesson; he/she is the lesson.

November 20

This morning I tried role play, a teaching technique I've seldom used. (Maybe I don't try different ways of teaching because I'm afraid they might fail.)

But this role play really succeeded, both in holding the class' interest and—more important—in advancing what we were studying.

We'd been thinking about the Christian person's attitude toward death, especially in the light of the ethics of the right to die. So I read a case study of a teen-age girl who suffered complete kidney failure and was on dialysis.

I asked different people in the class to take the parts of the girl, her parents, her younger sister, her physician and her pastor. The girl had separate conversations with each of these people about her desire to go off dialysis and be permitted to die.

Most of the people who played the roles matched the sexes and ages. But when it came to the girl's conversation with her doctor, I asked a physician who is part of the class and a young woman to take the parts—then switched the roles. (The real-life physician played the teen-age girl; the young woman played the physician.)

The high point was a conversation between the teenager and her younger sister. The two young women (college students) actually seemed to become the persons whose roles they had assumed. Mine weren't the only moist eyes after that particular role play. Talk about psychodrama!

We were as close as we could possibly come to such a heart-rending problem without actually experiencing it. And we understood the difficult emotional, relational and ethical considerations in far greater depth than would have been the case if I'd merely lectured.

November 21

One of the sharpest impressions I receive of Jesus as I read the accounts of His life and ministry in the Gospels is of His sensitivity.

It is said that He fulfilled an Old Testament prophecy: "A bruised reed shall he not break, and smoking flax shall he not quench . . ." (Matthew 12:20)

He is my model as a teacher. Therefore I must be sensitive to my students. I must perceive the reed that's bruised and not break it, the flax that's smoldering and not quench it.

Some students have the mere beginning of spiritual interest, even of Bible knowledge. I must be careful not to embarrass them by pushing them into discussions beyond their depth, by asking questions they cannot answer.

Other students hesitate to ask the question that's on their minds. How beautifully Jesus dealt with such people; he answered the unasked question—sometimes later—and didn't say, "What you really want to know is . . ." or "Don't you really mean . . ."

A pastor was discussing a problem involving the high-school class in his church with me at a Sunday school convention.

"We've got the best possible man to teach those kids," he said. And when he explained the teacher's background, work, family and interests, I had to agree. "Yet we keep losing students from the class. It's about half the size it was when he took it over."

"Tell me more about the man," I said. "What's he like as a teacher? Have you seen him in action, if not in the teaching situation, then on the church board or somewhere else? What's your first impression of him?"

The pastor was silent for several moments. Then he said,

"I know the answer to the problem with his class. He's sarcastic. He can make you feel that big"—here he spread his thumb and index finger about an inch apart—"if you disagree with him or don't quite see things his way."

Teenagers are tender plants, easily wilted by a strong wind. A tender touch, a tender teacher is needed.

For adults too. And children.

November 26

Jim makes things interesting in class. He gets us to think, although I'm not sure that's his motive for what he does.

What he does is ask questions, sometimes shockers.

Like today. We were studying the account of Jesus walking on the water, and Jim said, "Did Jesus really have to walk on the water? Couldn't that have been an optical illusion?"

After a moment, from the other side of the room, Evelyn spoke up: "Why, that's heresy!" (A good discussion-stopper if there ever was one.)

I tried to redeem the situation, saying something like, "Now that you've named it, let's discuss it."

And we did. I've never been in on such a good discussion of miracles. The thinking of all of us was sharpened, because Jim asked the question in the first place.

Jim is a scientist. He finds it hard to believe. I can't help wishing he'd spend a tenth of the time studying the Bible and Christian books that he spends studying the books and journals of his field of specialization.

Maybe someday he will. But meanwhile, I'm glad he feels safe with the class, safe enough to bring up his doubts and problems. I'll have to talk to Evelyn—I'd hate for her to squelch him.

December 2

This has been a busy week for me. I've been on the road most of the week, and also had some difficult decisions to make at the office. It's hard to get my mind settled on the class tomorrow.

But I guess I don't have it quite so bad as Dwight L. Moody did a century ago, when he was on the road all week and still taught Sunday school on Sunday morning.

Moody traveled throughout the Middle West, selling shoes. (Come to think of it, there were no airplanes then, only slow, dirty trains and horse-drawn wagons. I guess some stagecoaches, too.)

But he always returned to Chicago by Saturday night, because he had established a Sunday school on the near north side of the river, an area of high crime and juvenile delinquency.

His evangelistic concern for the poor children and young people, who would not go into a church, led him to locate his Sunday school in a public hall above a city market.

"Sunday was a busy day for me then," Moody later recalled. "During the week I would be out of town as a commercial traveler, selling boots and shoes, but I would always manage to be back by Saturday night. Often it was late when I got to my room, but I would have to be up by six to get the hall ready for Sunday school. Every Saturday night a German society held a dance there, and I had to roll out beer kegs, sweep up sawdust, clean up generally, and arrange the chairs. I did not think it was right to hire this done on Sunday, so sometimes with the assistance of a scholar, and often without any, I would do it myself.

"This usually took most of the morning, and when it was done I would have to drum up the scholars and new boys

20

and girls." (One scholar later recalled: "My first recollection of Mr. Moody was peeping around the corner of the building in order to have him chase me and bring me into the school.")

"By the time two o'clock came," continued Moody, "we would have the hall full, and then I had to keep order while the speaker of the day led the exercise. We had to keep things going to keep up the children's interest. When school was over I visited absent scholars and found out why they were not at Sunday school, called on the sick, and invited the parents to attend the evening service." *(Chicago Tribune)*

If Moody could make it in those circumstances, so can I. In spite of the week I've been through.

December 4

I failed today.

The lesson didn't come off. I know it and the class knows it.

First, there was that tangent. I should have stuck to the lesson when Matt raised the question; I should have said, "Matt, if you want to, we can discuss that after class. Or sometime during the week. I want to get through the lesson, and I don't think enough people are bothered by that to justify taking the time to discuss it now."

I know, and Matt knows, that there are some questions that bother so many people that it's necessary to consider them in class, even if you never get back to the lesson. But this wasn't one of them.

So we wasted fifteen minutes. I mean, I wasted fifteen minutes.

Then I tried to cover everything in the lesson in the time that remained. I rushed through the material; I even said, "There's no time for questions" when Grace raised her hand.

I know I should have settled for getting the main point across. But I didn't. I had to dump the whole load because I'd prepared it.

Then the culmination of that miserable class session was when Frank disagreed with me and I cut him off. I could see people's heads jerk back.

I'll have to tell them I'm sorry next week. I hope they'll forgive me.

I hope You'll forgive me, Lord. Thanks.

December 25

I think Christmas Sunday should be a special time.

And it was special in the class this morning.

First, we had steaming coffee and Danish streudel, brought by Marge and Al, ready for us when we arrived. A Christmas tablecloth, plates, cups and napkins brightened the room and gave it a festal air.

Then we sang carols, several of them. Most of us don't get enough carol-singing during the Christmas holidays, I've found.

We prayed specially for missionaries who have been part of the class and are now serving in various parts of the world. Somehow this brought them closer to us. We also had special prayer for our children, and welcomed students who were home for the holidays.

For the lesson time, I interrupted the series I've been teaching, since today's lesson would have been unrelated to

Christmas. I don't hesitate to make such changes, because it's easy to get into a rut.

We read the Luke 2 Christmas passage. This is a supremely familiar chapter, yet I was interested—as I almost always am when we are in such a passage—at the fresh insight people had, the way the Holy Spirit got through to us in a new way.

I often ask the class, "What impresses you about this passage? How do you feel at this point in your life as you read it?" Their replies never fail to interest me, and enlighten all of us.

The written Word, like the Living Word who became flesh today, is of such depth that we can never exhaust its meaning. It is like an ocean, and we are always taking out fresh water in our sandpails.

When we left the building where our class meets, to cross the street for the worship service in the main church building, it had begun to snow. The ground was already white.

"Looks like we'll have a white Christmas after all," someone said.

Suddenly a small snowball hit me, and I saw our son, who had been waiting to go into the service with us, put his gloves back on.

"Merry Christmas!" he called with a big grin.

I just smiled.

Later, when we got home, I smeared him with a big snowball. All in the spirit of the holiday, of course.

January 2

When I was a boy, maybe nine or ten years old, I remember how my father helped me make a model of a house during Jesus' time for Sunday school. We spent hours planning the project, getting the wood, sawing it and nailing it together, sanding and painting it (gray, with black lines tracing the outlines of stones). We even had a little opening in the roof of the house, like the one through which his friends lowered the man, when they brought him to Jesus for healing.

I had a lot of fun with Dad, and learned through the project; the whole class benefited from it.

Sometimes I assign projects to members of the class I'm teaching now. Not construction projects, although that might not be a bad idea. Things like reports on books, what the Bible says about a certain subject.

When we studied Amos, which speaks of God's judgment on a nation that forgets the poor, I asked one man, a sociologist, to prepare a report on poverty in the United States. (When he gave the report, we discovered he'd concentrated on poverty in DuPage County, the county in which we live. That brought it home to all of us in a way that the whole country wouldn't.)

At the end of that series of lessons, I assigned a project to each member of the class: Bring in a project you intend to do personally, or as a family, to help poor people. It was exciting to see how creative and yet down-to-earth the projects were.

(Mary Lou, my wife, has our family on what seems to be a rather permanent extension of this project and one of the pastor's sermons: a "Third World Meal" each Wednesday night. That means a dinner of rice only. We're giving the money we save to a relief organization. I can't say our two teen-age boys are wildly enthusiastic about the idea.)

I'll have to think up more projects related to lessons. This takes time, which may be why I don't do it very often. But the results far exceed the investment of time, like a lot of things related to teaching a Sunday school class.

24

January 13

Frank, who's in my class, told me about his daughter Yvonne today. She's home for the Christmas holidays, with her husband and little boy.

Their family was pretty strong from a Christian standpoint while she was growing up, and so was the church. But she's gone through a period of doubt and rebelling.

Now she's on her way back, according to Frank.

He says that he came into the living room a couple of days ago and found her sitting alone, just sitting and rocking in a chair.

"What are you doing?" he asked.

"I'm forgiving people," his daughter replied. "I've learned that it's necessary for me to be healed of my memories, and forgiving people is a very important part of it.".

"Such as, forgiving whom?" her father asked.

"Well, I've just been forgiving a Sunday school teacher I had as a child."

"Why do you feel that you have to forgive her?"

"Because she forced a stupid curriculum on me and never hugged me."

That was twenty years ago, and I think there's been a big improvement in Sunday school curriculum materials since then—especially the ones we publish at David C. Cook. (Of course, I'm most concerned about them and familiar with them.) We know a lot more about how children learn, what parts of the Bible are most relevant to their daily needs, how to explain spiritual things through their daily experiences.

But they still need attention from the teacher, the sort of attention that says, "I like you. I don't just teach because I have to, I teach you because I like you." And if you like

25

someone you'll give them a hug once in a while.

I hope nobody has to sit and forgive me, or the way I teach sometime in the future.

January 15

It must have been about a year ago that John and Kathleen asked to say something to the class.

I had a hunch that they were going to tell about their daughter, Becky. I was right.

John was the one who told the story, one that I knew already, along with the pastor and a few others. But the class—and the church itself—had not previously been aware of the serious problem.

In a simple, straightforward way, John told how, nine months before, their fifteen-year-old daughter had run away from home. They notified the police and searched for her everywhere, without success.

Then, about a month ago, the police found her: living with prostitutes, addicted to hard drugs, in an evil part of Chicago.

Becky was really spaced out when they found her, but it was only after examination by a team of psychiatrists that John and Kathleen realized how seriously she had been damaged.

"They tell us she has to be put in a mental institution," John said, struggling for control. "She's so sick that they don't think she'll ever be able to leave. One of them even said it would be no help to visit her there—that perhaps we'd better just forget we ever had a daughter."

Then, after a moment of silence, John concluded: "We wanted to tell you about this so you'd pray with us. Becky's

26

in the institution now, but we know God can do anything. He can heal her, and we hope you'll pray with us that He will—in spite of what the doctors told us." John and Kathleen sat down.

The class was deeply moved. Someone stood up to pray; then others prayed too.

Like I said, that was about a year ago. And we've been praying ever since.

This morning John and Kathleen asked to say something again. Only this time the two of them were radiantly happy when John spoke.

"We want you to know that Becky came back home last week. They've discharged her from the state hospital as cured. And she really is. She's already back in school, and she'll even be getting a job. I think you can guess how we feel. We want to thank you for sharing our heavy burden, for praying for Becky."

Again people prayed, this time praising and thanking God.

And in my heart I thanked Him for a class that cares, a group of Christians with whom John and Kathleen felt safe in sharing such a heavy concern—safe from a judgmental attitude toward them, or Becky, or how they had raised Becky.

I had one other thought: "Ye have not because ye ask not."

January 22

I wonder if I really got through to the class with Jeremiah this morning. It's hard to know for sure.

Maybe I need to remind myself again of that story Donald Grey Barnhouse told. (What an outstanding Bible teacher he was—he had the gift, like C. S. Lewis, of creating fresh windows through which you could see the truth.)

According to Dr. Barnhouse, he was riding in a car with a friend when the subject of music came up.

"What's your favorite symphony?" the friend asked.

"Brahms' *First*" was Dr. Barnhouse's reply.

"How does it go?"

Dr. Barnhouse began to whistle the main theme of the symphony.

"Then suddenly," he recalled, "I was overcome with how ridiculous it was that I should be trying to communicate that great musical composition with my weak whistle.

"But by the wonder of the human brain, my weak whistle was changed in my friend's mind into the strings and percussion and brass of the full symphony orchestra."

Then he applied the experience to his teaching. "Every time I stand up to teach the Bible, I'm overcome with how ridiculous it is that I should be trying to communicate God's Word to the class.

"It would be hopeless, except for one thing: The Holy Spirit is in me, teaching through me; and He is also in the men and women in my class who listen. So He turns my weak little whistle into the full symphony of God's revelation in their minds and lives."

I guess I have to learn more about trusting the Holy Spirit to teach through me, and to receive and confirm the Word of God in my students. Including the Book of Jeremiah.

January 29

Late this afternoon I sat at my office desk and thought about the members of my class. The day was dull gray; snow was starting to fall in the little avenue outside my window.

I'd finished all my correspondence and the reports of the day; I'd seen my last associate. In less than an hour I'd be leaving for home.

My desk was clean, except for the small lamp.

So I imagined the members of my class, some of them, walking across the desk. In my imagination they were little people; they took little steps, so it took each a half-minute or so to move from one side to the other.

There's Norm, alone. I wish Dorothy were with him; they're living mostly apart, she at some distance. They're both such great people; they'll need each other more and more as they get older. *Lord, help them to give in to each other, to find the joy of living together, doing your things together rather than their own thing apart.*

Bart and Elsie. So concerned about their grown kids, living at such a distance from the Lord—and from them. How can kids be so cruel? Why did their Christian upbringing have so little effect? *Lord, I don't have to understand, to diagnose the situation. I want to bring Bart and Elsie with their hurt to you, and I want to bring their children to you.*

Dear Jenny. So faithful to the Lord and to all her responsibilities as a school teacher. And so alone, with her family a thousand miles away. We'll have to see if she can come over for the afternoon some Sunday soon. *Thank You for such a consistent Christian and interesting person, Lord.*

Here comes Martha. Last Sunday she asked us to pray for her; she's taking the exams for her registered nurse qualification this week. And I forgot. *Lord, help Martha have a clear mind so she'll remember what she's studied during the past several years. Give her the assurance of your presence now and your concern for her future plans.*

Florence. How she must miss Arthur. It's about a year since his sudden, unexpected death. She's had so many loose ends to gather together and she's done it so well. *Help Florence in her loneliness, Lord. You've promised to be a husband to the widow and a father to the fatherless. Carry out your promise to her and to Art. He's just entering adolescence, she's raising him alone, and she needs your help.*

I turned around to look out the window. The snow was falling much harder. I thought I'd better leave if I was going to get home—the hill by Villa Olivia would really be crowded with cars and semis, and some would probably be stuck.

Goodbye for now, Lord. Bless the whole class with their needs, and me with mine.

February 3

Martha passed her exams and will soon be an R.N. She could hardly wait until we had sung the hymns and the leader asked for any prayer requests or praise items, to speak up and tell us.

We were all excited along with her. After all, we had prayed her through those exams.

"You're like my extended family," she said.

An extended family: that's what our class is all about. A safe place for Martha and the rest of us. And God's the head of the family.

February 12

At the Boise, Idaho Sunday school convention last week, a teacher asked me, "What do you do when you ask a question and nobody answers?"

My first suggestion was that after giving the class time to respond, I go on with the lesson, leaving the question unanswered. The minute you begin answering your own questions, I told her, you're lost. After a few times, the class never will respond. They'll think all your questions are rhetorical, that you don't expect answers.

On the other hand, if you just go on with your teaching, leaving the question unanswered, they'll know you mean business.

Of course, I said, you have to be sure that the questions you ask aren't too easy, or the answers too obvious. Children will answer such questions, but teenagers won't.

An occasional teen-age class—not adults, usually—will refuse to respond to questions or participate in discussion, regardless of what you do. I once had such a class of senior highs and was quite discouraged by my inability to break through to them.

I talked the problem over with a skilled professional schoolteacher whose answer made me feel better: "The same thing happens to us who teach all the time. The first period of the day, you'll have a class that is fairly bursting with responses. You can hardly keep them quiet. Then along comes the second-period class. There's no perceptible difference in size or makeup of class from the first-period one, and they sit on their hands. You can't get any response at all. It's one of the mysteries of teaching."

Her answer comforted me. But I did one thing that finally worked with that class: I told them that I was setting aside the last ten minutes of class for any questions they might want to ask. The questions might arise out of what we had studied, but they didn't have to.

That idea really worked. My silent class began to talk, and I was no longer in the dark about their understanding of the lessons, or their needs.

But they never did answer questions or discuss things in the main class period.

February 18

I've been thinking about how Jesus worked as a carpenter from the time he was a child until the age of thirty, when He entered upon His "mission," His public ministry.

Almost half of His parables were about business and ordinary work, about the "life that is so daily."

When He called men to be His disciples, He didn't call them from religious vocations. Instead He called fishermen, tradesmen, government employees. And He told them to teach people what He had taught them.

He still calls business people and homemakers, doctors, nurses and lawyers, government employees, school teachers and fishermen, farmers and welders and scientists and construction workers, and tells us to teach boys and girls, teens and adults what He has taught us.

We can't turn Him down (or turn down the Sunday school superintendent, pastor, or director of Christian education who confronts us with His call) with the excuse that we haven't had formal religious training. If we do, we'll miss out as surely as Peter, John, and Matthew would have missed out if they had refused His call.

February 23

I must teach tomorrow morning, and I've left my preparation until tonight. It's already after eleven o'clock; maybe I should go to bed and set the alarm so I'll get up early. Then I can study with a fresher mind.

This has been a busy week. A lot of unexpected things came up at the office and here at home. These and other rationalizations fill my mind.

But I got the other things done; why did I put off preparing the Sunday school lesson I'll have to teach tomorrow morning?

It mustn't have seemed as important as the other things. I know enough about the Bible that maybe I felt I could get by without the preparation I needed for the other things.

Whatever the reason, I'm stuck. I can't even pray for God's help with a clear conscience, because it's my fault I'm stuck.

I'll set the alarm.

Maybe you'd better set it tomorrow night.

Why? The class is tomorrow morning; it will be all over tomorrow night.

Set the alarm to remind you to begin studying for the following Sunday.

But that's a whole week away.

Ten minutes each day is a lot better than sixty minutes on Saturday night or Sunday morning.

I guess that's right. But what should I do each day?

Read the Bible passage you'll be teaching. Read it through once or twice each day. Pray that you'll understand it.

That sounds like something I read about called unconscious learning.

And that's what it is. You'll be thinking about those verses

33

and your class all week; you'll be steeped in them by the time Sunday comes.

Right. What else should I do?

Read the teacher's guide. Mark it. See if there are any illustrations or applications that should be changed for your class. Your class is unique, you know.

Don't I know it.

So is every class. The editor in Elgin, Illinois can't possibly know all these classes the way their teachers know them. So teachers have to tailor-make the lesson for the class.

What else should I do?

Set your alarm for six o'clock tomorrow morning.

I don't need that much time to prepare. I don't need to get up that early.

Have you prayed for your class this week?

Well . . .

Set your alarm. Now. And pray to be forgiven for taking your teaching responsibilities so lightly, for failing to set the right priorities.

March 4

I taught a series of lessons on death and the Christian a few months ago.

Today Bruce came up to me after class and said, "I want you to know that those lessons on death you taught some time ago have changed my whole attitude.

"I've had a series of tests at the hospital this past week, tests that could reveal something pretty serious.

"I don't know the results yet, but the surprising thing is that I'm at peace. I've found I can really trust God. So I wanted to thank you."

March 11

A young woman who's working on her doctorate in psychology recently told me about her research project.

She's investigating the importance of eye contact, looking directly into a person's eyes when talking to him or listening to him.

Somehow, she said, this communicates a number of different impressions: concern, interest, attention, acceptance, sometimes affection.

I've thought about this young psychologist's words in connection with teaching. I've come to several conclusions.

One is that I must know the lesson well enough to look at people while I'm teaching, instead of having my eyes mainly looking downward at a book or notes.

Another is that I must look directly into the eyes of a student who's responding, give him/her my undivided attention. This says, "You're important; you're why I'm teaching."

Still another is that if I ask a question and no one answers, I must look at the class rather than look down or away in embarrassment at the silence. Looking into their eyes will indicate that I expect an answer, that I'm not uptight over the period of silence.

As the teacher, I set the tone for the class. In this as in other situations, if I'm not embarrassed or uptight, the class won't be either. If I am, they'll be.

Men, women, children, important people, little people, traitors, sinners: Everybody felt at home with Jesus because He never put them down; He gave Himself totally to each individual. He sincerely wanted each one to realize the potential of his/her life.

March 17

Someone passed the following quotation on to me, from a graffiti wall at St. John's University in Minnesota:

"Jesus said to them, 'Who do you say that I am?'

"And they replied, 'You are the eschatological manifestation of the ground of our being, the kerygma in which we find the ultimate meaning of our interpersonal relationships.'

"And Jesus said, 'What?' "

I like that.

I like it because it sets the simplicity of our Lord's words and teaching over against the complexity of some technical expressions of truth.

Not that theology is wrong. We need deep thinkers who can explain the ramifications of our faith.

But such complexity of ideas belongs in a seminary classroom, not on the hillside where Jesus taught multitudes, or in the room where I teach my Sunday school class.

Jesus was profound, but simple in expression. Ordinary people heard Him gladly, eagerly.

To use an old but true way of expressing it, He put the cookies—or the bread of life—on the lowest shelf, where anyone could reach it.

And so must I.

I cannot show off my knowledge (the little that I have) or my vocabulary and still teach as Jesus taught. Nor get through to people as He got through to them.

What expression of truth could be more simple than that contrast at the conclusion of the Sermon on the Mount between the man who built his house on the rock and the man who built his house on the sand.

I have a few professors and medical doctors in my class. I

could become threatened by their presence, overwhelmed by the impossibility of my measuring up to their standards of scholarly teaching.

That I'm neither threatened nor overwhelmed is the result of knowing that Ph.D.s and M.D.s have the same feelings I have: they bleed when they're cut; they grieve when their children go into a far country, away from parents and the Lord. And they have the same God, the same Bible, the same life in Christ.

One more thing gives me confidence as I teach. I believe these learned people come to Sunday school for the same reason as the rest of us: to learn about God and have fellowship with His people, our brothers and sisters in Christ. They appreciate simple truth.

But when I run into a question I can't answer, it's great to have such resource people around.

March 26

The young adult (singles) group had their Easter sunrise service at our home this morning. This is the third year they've been here, and we hope they'll make it a tradition.

Actually "sunrise" is wishful thinking, since the sun was well up when they got here.

Last year Easter was later and they could meet outside, sitting on blankets. Today there is still snow on the ground, so they crowded into our living room and country kitchen.

They sang Easter songs and laughed happily and read the Bible and prayed and talked about the meaning of Easter to them and laughed happily and sang some more, while Mary Lou and I did the final work on breakfast in the kitchen. We could hear everything and see part of the group.

I don't know whether the smell of coffee perking and sausage frying had any effect or not, but their service didn't last long. Soon the happy group had overflowed into the kitchen and they were helping take the egg-and-cheese souffle and coffee cakes out of the oven, and everyone was filling cups and plates. The coffee cakes were brought by the young adults, some of whom had made them. One of the most delicious was made by a young man; I wonder, will he ever get married?

Martha shared the secret of her impending engagement with Mary Lou and me before she left. We're so glad for her.

Believe it or not, we got the dishes finished and the place straightened up before we left for Sunday school. Our own class was sort of an anticlimax, and a sleepy one at that.

March 29

Phil took his own life this week.

Nineteen years old, studying music at the state university, an accomplished cellist, a warm human being who was liked by everybody who knew him: Phil stepped in front of a freight train last Wednesday night.

His parents are in my class. So was Phil, when he was home from school.

Why didn't I see that something was wrong? Why didn't I arrange to spend time with Phil outside of class? Did I look at him as an extension of his parents instead of a person with his own independent life and needs?

The funeral will be hard. So will class next Sunday morning. Everybody is hurting.

I hope we hurt enough to change, to really care for each other—especially the lonely ones—as Jesus cares.

April 2

Phil's parents seemed to be absent from class this morning. Actually his mother was there, although she was sitting behind someone and I didn't see her.

So thinking neither one was there, I suggested that we pray for them and their other children before I started to teach. It was a time of warm, specific praying.

Afterward, when I was about ten minutes into the lesson, I saw her. My mind formed one of those flashes of prayer while someone else was talking, "Lord, help Betty to understand our love for them and not to be hurt by being singled out in that prayer."

The class was subdued for the whole teaching time. I'm sure Phil was on all our minds—beautiful, outgoing, seemingly happy Phil. The seat he'd never fill again.

About fifteen minutes before I was finished teaching, Betty quietly left the room. This really troubled me. Had the prayer, the atmosphere of the class, been too much for her? Again I prayed, "Lord, be with Betty. Help her know we love her."

I was under the burden right through the church worship service that followed.

After the service, Betty came up to me.

"I'm sorry I had to leave the class early. I'd promised to help with the nursery, and felt I should go through with it . . . in spite of what happened last week. And thank you for praying for us at the beginning of class. It means so much to know that the class is standing with us."

My heart sang. Not like a dove on a summer night; more like a sparrow on a cold, snowy day in the dead of winter.

How easy it is to misunderstand, to come to wrong conclusions.

39

April 11

I have to remember that I'm an authority figure to the class. I may try to preserve a low profile, ask others for their opinions, be tentative rather than "Now hear this," but I can't really escape it.

I may not escape it, but I can try not to foster it.

The authority in any Sunday school class, including mine, is the Bible—not the teacher. I have to turn people to the Word of God rather than to my personal opinions.

I do have opinions that I occasionally share with the class. But I try to remember to say immediately afterward, "If you disagree with me, the Lord bless you. You may be right and I may be wrong."

On the other hand, when I have a "Thus saith the Lord"—something the Bible clearly says—I indicate its authority, to which both I as teacher and the class must submit.

The trouble comes, it seems to me, when a teacher confuses his/her own opinions with the Word of God, and teaches both with equal authority.

In later years (and this is a special danger when teaching teens and young adults), if members of the class discover that the teacher was wrong in the personal opinions he taught with such authority, they are likely to discard the Bible he taught as well.

I also think we teachers should be careful to teach from the Bible, not from a teacher's guide, or at least read the Bible passage directly from the Bible and have it open throughout the class session. This makes the Bible's authority clear to the class.

I often outline what the teacher's guide says, and put the outline alongside my Bible, to reinforce this. An added advantage is that I am forced to express the lesson in my own words, and am not tempted just to read from the teacher's guide.

But because I can't escape the authority of my position as teacher, I must be sensitive to what people say and how I respond.

Like last Sunday, when Ron, who hasn't come very often, gave that far-out opinion during the discussion. I knew that he'd feel it pretty keenly if I told him he was wrong. So instead I said to the class, "How do the rest of you feel? Do you agree with Ron?" And they handled it.

Of course I could have asked Ron, "Where do you find that in the passage we're studying?" and it wouldn't have been quite so bad as telling him he was wrong in front of everybody. But I still think it was better to let the class respond. They're his peers—I, the teacher, am not, even though I try not to be authoritarian.

April 15

We had a great time of sharing concerns and praying for each other at the beginning of class this morning.

I think the class would continue to meet, even if there were no lesson. We've found out that we can depend on each other, that we can trust each other, that we can be open with each other.

I guess one thing we've found out is that we're not alone with our problems. Other Christians have the same ones, whether it's older children who have gotten away from the Lord, relatives who are seriously ill, loss of employment, final exams, important decisions, personal or family crises of various kinds.

This week I had a letter from a woman in another part of the country. That letter made me realize what a priceless treasure we have in our class' warm fellowship.

"Last year I passed through a severe depression and felt so strongly the need to be able to discuss my problem with people who would 'really' pray for me and with me—people who cared enough to share my agony. I think of my church as being a friendly place and it is really my family, since I have no Christian relatives . . . Now that God has supplied a victory over this, I can share it to a certain extent; but even now, I feel embarrassment on the part of listeners. I'm certain that shared prayer would have helped me through this time much faster.

"During my own infirmity, a young couple of the church separated—the wife left her husband to return to her parents in another state. The young man broke down in a Wednesday night prayer meeting and asked for prayer, saying that he had examined himself before God and thought that he was doing everything he knew to make things right with her. But he wanted the people to pray for their reunion. Again, I felt strong embarrassment on the part of the congregation and lack of deep caring. The church is his only family, too. My distress for him was made worse when the only comments I heard later were that he should have known better than to speak of such a private affair in a public service."

Thank God we can speak of "private affairs" in our Sunday school class. I think every church needs such safe places, places of refuge and Christian concern and support.

April 21

I can't explain it.

Sometimes there are three or four hands in the air at once. (My class is too large for students just to speak out.) Then I'm pretty sure the lesson is making people think and respond.

Other times there are no hands. I ask a question and nobody answers.

Of course it may be the question I've asked. Teens and adults won't usually respond to "where" or "who" or "what" questions: Where did Moses go when he left Egypt? Who sentenced Shadrach, Meshach and Abednego to the fiery furnace? What verse in today's text tells us not to worry?

The answer is there in the Bible in front of everybody, so why should anyone bother to respond?

I have to admit that when I've booby-trapped myself with such a question, a dear older person often rescues me by answering. But it's obvious to the class that I'm the recipient of an act of Christian charity.

I've found that the questions that get results start with "how" and "why."

Like "How do you think Moses felt when his own people turned on him and refused his help?" Or "Why shouldn't we worry about the future?"

When I ask that sort of question, I'm making people think, expecting them to think. I'm letting them put things together in their own heads.

In my opinion, people of all ages (not just adults) like to discover things for themselves, rather than be limited to what the teacher says. When I ask a "how" or "why" question, I open up this possibility to my class.

There's another question I like to ask. It's this: "Have any of you had a similar experience?" For instance, "to what

Moses had when his own people rejected him"?

Why should the class be limited to my perceptions, my feelings, my experiences,when they have equally authentic ones to share? And when someone does share, his/her experience will probably speak to members of the class who can't relate as well to my age or lifestyle or background.

Today I asked the right kind of questions and the class still sat on their hands. I gave them the opportunity to share their own thoughts and experiences, and only one or two responded.

Maybe it was just the rainy Sunday doldrums. It's a miserable gray day.

Or am I rationalizing?

April 30

In its beginnings two centuries ago, and for more than half of its history, Sunday school was primarily evangelistic.

That's why it was held on Sunday afternoon, rather than—as in this century—before church on Sunday morning.

Children whose own parents did not attend church were thus attracted, and many put their trust in Jesus Christ. Most children of church people, on the other hand, did not attend. Instead they went with their parents to the morning worship service.

A great change took place early in the present century, when Sunday school was moved to the morning hour and children from church homes began to attend.

This changed the nature of Sunday school from an instrument of evangelism to one of Christian education. It did something else: parents who had previously taught their children the Bible and Christian doctrine (often through the catechism) at home turned this responsibility over to the Sunday school. Family altar (Bible reading and prayer) was dropped in most church homes.

I think we have to be aware of this bit of history if we are to understand two urgent needs in the Sunday school's ministry today.

The first is the need for a fresh emphasis on evangelism. Christian education begins with Christian people, whether children, teenagers or adults, who have trusted Jesus Christ and committed their lives to Him.

The bus ministry of many churches is similar to the original evangelistic emphasis of Sunday school.

But we also need fresh attention to evangelizing children from church homes. Without family Bible reading and prayer, their need for a clear explanation of the gospel and opportunity to respond cannot be forgotten. But it often is.

I know a teacher of junior boys whom I admire because he is aware of this need and is doing something about it.

Each fall, when he gets a new class, this young man takes the boys—one at a time—for Saturday morning breakfast at a pancake house. Over this breakfast, he tries to find out the boy's relationship to God and to lead him to faith in Christ if he is uncertain.

I need to have this same concern for my class.

The second urgent need of today's Sunday school is to impress upon church parents the need for Christian education in the home, and to train them to provide this education. God gave Christian parents primary responsibility for their own children's spiritual training, not the church or Sunday school.

The Christian home and Sunday school make a great team.

May 3

We got into a discussion of Christian business ethics in class today. I was reminded of something that happened ten years or so ago at a small college in Virginia, when I was invited to speak at religious emphasis week (which the students irreverently but accurately called "Let's be kind to God week").

I was at a fraternity house for dinner, with a voluntary-attendance discussion on religion in the lounge afterward. Most of the men stayed for the discussion, and there was a lot of interest in the Christian gospel.

After about two hours, they thanked me, said goodbye and went back to their studies—all except a rather intense young man. He was one of the few who hadn't said anything earlier.

When we were alone, he introduced himself and said, "I used to believe everything you told us tonight. I could have presented my faith as clearly as you did. But all that ended the summer after my senior year in high school."

"What happened then?" I asked.

"I had this Sunday school teacher my senior year. He was a really good teacher, and we learned a lot from him. He was a leader in the church.

"That summer, before I entered school here, I got a job in our small city. On that job I learned that this great Sunday school teacher was despised by the business community for his ethics. He was in on all the shady deals, it seemed.

"Well, I decided if that's the way Christians lived, I didn't want any of it. If he could talk so great in Sunday school and live so lousy during the week, his religion wasn't for me."

I reasoned with him: his faith should rest in Jesus Christ, the perfect Lord and Savior, not in any businessman or

Sunday school teacher. I told him about Christian leaders I had known who were exemplary businessmen: H. J. Taylor of Club Aluminum, Dave Weyerhaeuser of the West Coast lumber company, Bob Swanson of New York's Thomas Bread Company.

To no avail.

He left, and although I saw him again toward the end of the week, he gave no indication of any change of mind.

It's not enough for me to claim to be a Christian, to be able to give a clear statement of my faith.

I must be trying to live up to my high calling as a Christian in Christ Jesus. And that includes my ethics as a businessman.

There's a danger in "talking further down the road than you've walked," as Vance Havner put it. It's dangerous for me, and it's dangerous for my students.

"If any man's life at home is unworthy," Charles Haddon Spurgeon said before the introduction of the automobile, "let him go ten miles away from home before he stands up to teach." Today he'd say a couple of hundred miles.

"Then, when he stands up," Spurgeon concluded, "let him say nothing."

May 16

I've been sitting here thinking about Bruce's encouraging words one Sunday about the lessons on death. Actually, his phone call telling me that everything's okay started me thinking.

Teaching adults has one distinct advantage over teaching other age groups, that members of your class occasionally mention help they've received from the lesson. Not just

Bruce, but others. Steven is such an encouragement to me—he's a good Bible teacher, but so often he expresses appreciation for things I've said in class.

I remember teaching junior and senior highs. They never said anything; I was forced to operate in the dark.

In the dark? No, I guess I mean, by faith. Faith that God was using my teaching even though I had no feedback from the class.

I like feedback, especially when it's complimentary. But I have to remember that this isn't the primary indication that God is working.

I also have to remember that sometimes God's Word hurts. As that great missionary to India, Amy Carmichael put it, "If you have never been hurt by a word from God, it is probable that you have never heard God speak."

May 18

At regular intervals I pick up a newspaper or magazine and read an obituary of the Sunday school.

In ten years, says the spokesman for a major church body in a typical interview, projecting present losses of students, the Sunday school will be dead, an extinct species.

These articles depress me until I go to Sunday school and see the interest people still have in studying the Bible; or to a Sunday school convention and see the interest other people have in becoming better prepared to teach the Bible. (Such conventions have greatly increased in number and size in recent years.)

Studying the Bible and teaching the Bible: there's the key, in my opinion. Sunday schools that are centered in the Word of God are seldom losing students; many of them are growing dramatically. On the other hand, it's not surprising that schools that have turned from the Bible and are concentrating on psychological and sociological studies are losing ground.

People want bread, not a stone. They want to hear about Jesus. And they want their children to find the road that leads to life—especially in these years when there are so many other roads that lead to frustration and death.

I can't believe that an institution that has 46 million students and four million teachers is dying. Rather, it seems to be one of the few hopeful signs on the horizon in the United States and Canada.

"When the enemy shall come in like a flood, the Spirit of the Lord shall lift up a standard against him." (Isaiah 59:19) This seems to be a principle illustrated in Western civilization during the past two centuries by the Sunday school.

Whether in late eighteenth-century England, with all its immorality and callousness toward children, when Robert Raikes started the first Sunday school; in nineteenth-century America, when the period of Westward expansion was at its height—and Sunday schools were being founded in new communities from the Mississippi to the Pacific, schools that later grew into churches; in the crisis of the War Between the States; in Chicago after the great fire, when Dwight L. Moody and David C. Cook were establishing Sunday schools in that devastated city: Sunday school has always proved to be a standard raised by the Spirit of God in periods of crisis.

Can it be different today, when the enemy of our souls and the souls of our children has come in like a new and terrible flood, with waves of materialism, of anarchy, of moral relativism?

I think not.

At the time of the communist takeover in China, when Christians were going through a period of severe testing and

49

imprisonment—another kind of Satanic flood—someone made the statement, "Christians are like tea. It takes hot water to bring out the best in them."

I think Sunday school is like that too.

May 21

Last Thursday night, Mary Lou and I attended an appreciation dinner put on by our church for the Sunday school staff. It was a nice evening; the food was especially good. (At potluck suppers, I think it would be a good idea to have a card in front of each dish: "Prepared by—or created by—" followed by the name of the person. Then you could express your appreciation to the right person for that extra-special salad mold. Also, it would probably upgrade the food.)

The speaker was good, too. But one question he asked bothered me. It was, "Do you ever get impatient with the stupid questions people ask during class?"

After we got home, I said to Mary Lou, "You know, I can't recall ever being asked a stupid question in class."

She couldn't either, from her experience teaching children.

"I've heard some stupid answers," I told her, "and given some. But no stupid questions."

It's such a delight to have a student ask you to clarify something he doesn't understand, even though the rest of the class does understand it. Or to express a doubt that you—and the class—can help resolve, because she had the courage to bring it out into the open. Or to ask how to deal with some problem of Christian lifestyle.

If I respect the students I teach, I'll respect their questions.

May 26

"I hear, I forget; I see, I remember; I do, I understand."

I don't know who said that, but whoever it was, he/she knew a lot about teaching.

It's so easy for me to limit myself to lecturing when I teach, to aim the lesson at ear-gate alone.

Jesus didn't make this mistake. He did lecture—the Sermon on the Mount is a beautiful example of this. But he used other teaching methods as well.

He told stories that were aimed at the heart. Who can forget the prodigal son (and his older brother), the lost sheep, the good Samaritan, the poor widow and an unjust judge?

And sometimes He left those stories open-ended. He didn't explain what they meant, but left the members of His class to figure them out for themselves.

I think we'd be better teachers today if we left some things open-ended, if we confronted our students with the nagging attempt to discover elusive truth. Why do we have to hit people over the head with the truth every time? There's joy in personal discovery.

He also wrote in the sand on at least one occasion. I guess that's next best to a chalkboard or overhead projector. Such an extension of teaching certainly makes more of an impression than spoken words alone.

Jesus used object lessons. It almost seems sacrilegious to refer to the Lord's Supper as an object lesson, but that's what it was, and still is.

He took the elements of an ordinary meal—bread and wine—and used them to impress the truth of His death for our sins indelibly upon our minds.

Could the disciples ever forget the lesson of their Lord, kneeling before them to wash their feet, the night He was betrayed?

He also carried on dialogs with individuals, both to teach the one with whom He spoke and also to teach the larger group who listened in. And the larger group did not merely learn from Jesus' words; they also learned from His attitude toward the other person. Love and respect and acceptance were doubtless communicated in this way.

How did the disciples know that Jesus loved the rich young ruler (Mark 10:21)? He didn't say He did; in fact, what He said to the young man resulted in his turning away from following Jesus.

I think it was Jesus' attitude toward him that convinced the disciples.

And the class observes my attitude toward the people with whom I carry on a dialog, especially if they don't automatically follow what I say.

June 12

"I do, I understand." It's when people actually do something that the lesson is finally grasped.

Hearing and seeing are essential to learning, but doing seems to be the test. "If you know these things," Jesus said, "happy are you if you do them."

And for three years Jesus was involved with His disciples in the doing.

He didn't just teach them the elements of prayer; He prayed with them. He didn't give them principles of witnessing; they listened as He confronted men and women with the necessity to believe. He didn't just tell them they ought to be compassionate; they observed His compassion.

And then He sent them out, two by two, to do it on their own.

When I was a high-school student, I had a Sunday school teacher who taught us the Bible on Sunday morning, but also taught us how to do it other nights of the week.

This teacher was a busy medical doctor, but he and his wife (they had no children at the time) took the class to New York City rescue missions to hold meetings. We learned that the Spirit of God was able to use even our weak words to deliver hopeless alcoholics. They took us to busy corners to hold street meetings, where we learned boldness in giving a Christian testimony to those who often opposed us or belittled us.

Today, more than forty years later, I continue to benefit from those lessons in doing.

It's harder to involve adults in doing, but it's possible. Maybe Sunday school classes should be the center for doing in the church, rather than a lot of other isolated interest groups. This would certainly provide for natural follow-through and prayer support.

Two weeks ago we had an example of doing. And Ray told us of the results in class today.

Ray heads up an organization that provides assistance to medical missionaries overseas. He told us during the prayer time in that earlier class session about one of India's outstanding evangelists who needs a kidney transplant if he's to continue to live. The kidney is available, he said; the money for medical expenses is not. He wanted the class to pray about this need.

We did pray. Then, when I got up to teach, I said, "Do you think that God may be speaking to us about meeting this need? If you do, and if you want to help without affecting your regular giving to the church or the church's missionary budget, leave money or a check with Doug (one of the class members) before you leave."

Today Ray told us how much has come in from the class during the past couple of weeks: two thousand dollars. Almost enough, he says, for the life-extending surgery on this man of God in India.

It's exciting to do things together . . . for the glory of God.

June 19

When I stop to think about it, one of the most exciting things about teaching Sunday school is that I'm building the church: the church of which I'm a part today, and the church of my children and grandchildren tomorrow.

Without men and women grounded in the Word of God and in Christian doctrine, the church would fall apart—or, perhaps worse, become a shadow of what our Lord intended, even a caricature.

Where do these men and women become thus grounded? In Sunday school, usually from the time they are little children.

"Whom shall he teach knowledge? And whom shall he make to understand doctrine? Them that are weaned from the milk, and drawn from the breasts. For precept must be upon precept, precept upon precept; line upon line, line upon line; here a little, and there a little." (Isaiah 28: 9, 10) This is the Bible's own description of the process, which begins with preschoolers and continues to old age.

And my class is part of the process. I'm part of it.

June 21

In the pre-lesson part of our class (I dislike the term "opening exercises"—it sounds like doing the knee-bends), the leader asks anyone who has a first-time guest to introduce him/her or if a person has come without being brought by a regular attender, to introduce himself. (Even in the latter instance someone sitting next to the newcomer often has found out who the person is and makes the introduction.)

These introductions are brief and low-key. The person doesn't stand up, and isn't embarrassed or put on the spot too much.

If they're newcomers to the community, George (our class president, who has a friendly manner that puts people at ease, despite the fact he is a lawyer) may ask where they live or work—then mention someone else in the class who lives or works in the same place.

There's a family feeling in class. At times someone needs special affirmation—and receives it. Or someone has done something special, or the child of a class member has achieved some honor or goal. Then there is recognition, and the whole class rejoices. If someone has been away, he is usually welcomed back. This includes children who came home from college or the service.

We have some Christian workers in the class. Two sisters went to the Far East to teach, and we prayed for them at home each morning (at least the ones we remembered) when we put on our shoes.

Requests for prayer aren't just remembered in class; they become part of many members' prayer lists for the next week or longer.

We're like a family, the family of God in this place.

June 23

This morning Herb had too much to say again.

I tried to overlook him when he raised his hand repeatedly to answer questions, or to volunteer insights.

His contributions are usually good, because he really knows the Bible. I wish I knew as much of it by memory as he does! (Maybe I'd better get started on a Bible memory plan, if for no other reason, to prove I still can learn.)

And Herb is eager for the return of our Lord Christ. His gaze is fixed on that happy hope—and he frequently reminds us of it. I like that. It brings us back to Christian reality.

But sometimes Herb's a problem, like this morning.

Most of the people in the class know about the automobile accident he had a few years ago, that cut his brilliant career in engineering short. We all love Herb and his wife.

But it's not good for the class when one person tends to monopolize things. And I don't think it's good for Herb, either.

I've tried to do something about it. A couple of times I've said, after class when we were alone, "Herb, you and I know a lot about the Bible. We have to be quiet sometimes and give other people a chance to respond to questions."

And I've tried to let Elaine know that I'm not uptight about it, and that I'm sure the class isn't either.

Maybe that's all I can do. Maybe the class needs the example of my loving acceptance of Herb and respect for his ideas more than it needs opportunities for more people to answer questions.

July 5

Vacation time. People are away, the class was smaller than usual.

And the room was stuffy, in spite of the fan I brought along this morning.

I hope something got through to the class. They must have had a hard time concentrating on the lesson; I know I would have, if I hadn't been teaching.

What was the lesson about this morning? Nothing new to that group of people, or to me either, for that matter.

I remember, years ago, reading about an older woman—a Christian of many years—who thanked her pastor for what his recent sermons had meant to her, one Sunday as she left the service.

She said it quickly, and was about to move away after shaking his hand.

"Thank you," the pastor said. "What did you find helpful in last Sunday's message?"

"I don't remember," the woman said.

Somewhat crestfallen, the pastor said, "How about the week before that?"

Again, "I don't remember." Then, as the pastor was turning from her, she said, "You know, pastor, it's like putting a colander under the water to wash it when it's dirty. The colander doesn't retain the water, but it gets cleansed in the process. When you teach me God's Word, I may not remember what you said, but I get cleansed and renewed by it."

Thank you, God, that even when the lesson isn't exciting, even when the students can't remember what I said, Your Holy Spirit can use it in their lives. Just let me teach Your Word and have faith in You. Amen.

July 12

I'm glad Kenny is in the class. He's God's special gift to all of us.

His bright smile and "Hi, Joe," as he hands me a hymnbook at the door, start the hour off just right.

How much does he understand of the complicated ideas we pass back and forth, teacher to student, student to teacher, student to student?

Very little, I'm sure.

But he understands that Jesus loves him, that his parents, brothers and sisters love him (they have for more than thirty years), and that the class loves him.

I remember the Sunday we sang "Happy Birthday to Kenny": his smile almost exploded off his face.

Sometimes when I speak to him after class he points to his necktie, his shoes or some other article of clothing, letting me know they're new.

By his faithful attention to giving out the hymnbooks before class, and turning out the lights afterward, Kenny teaches the teacher.

But he teaches me something more. Sometimes when I'm teaching, my eyes light upon Kenny, sitting there in the first row, taking notes (regular up and down lines in a notebook).

Then I think, "God, help me and the whole class to see you with Kenny's simple faith and love. Move us beyond the clutter of complicated ideas to yourself."

"The last shall be first," Jesus said. Maybe in heaven I'll be studying under Kenny's teaching.

July 17

Alfred North Whitehead, the great educator, described enthusiasm as "the extra spurt of energy that drives a buzz-saw through the knots in a log."

I find that I must be enthusiastic if I'm to carry the class along with me through the lesson. They seem to know when I enjoy teaching; then they enjoy learning. When I don't, they don't.

This morning I was teaching a lesson that I wasn't particularly enthusiastic about. Maybe I should have substituted something else, but I don't like to break the continuity.

I prayed that I'd have enthusiasm anyway.

Then I stood up to teach (sometimes I sit down; the desk has a lectern on it, so I can choose), and I suddenly realized that these people were waiting to hear the Word of God. They had come to hear God's voice, not mine.

Suddenly I felt enthusiastic—not for the lesson, but for those people in my class. And above all, for the awesome privilege that was mine to teach them God's Word.

It was a good lesson.

I've found that sometimes a student rescues the situation with his/her enthusiasm. This seems to occur most frequently with those who have recently come to faith in Jesus Christ, to knowledge of the freedom He brings to living.

You can't manufacture enthusiasm. But you can pray that God will give it—through the teacher or through a student.

August 12

It's late. The class went to Hansens' for a "sing" tonight, after church.

Their apartment is 18 floors up, and in the middle of the sing a sudden, violent storm arose to the northeast.

The lights went out for a brief time, and we crowded the windows and small balcony to observe the lightning flashes and hear the thunder claps.

As someone said, the power of God is so obvious during a storm, whether it's over the ocean or over the prairie.

Then the lights went back on and—as suddenly as it had begun—the storm ended and a heavy rain began.

We found our seats again, and Bob finally got the group quiet.

"Tonight we're saying goodbye to Eileen," he said. "She'll be returning to her teaching in Singapore. We'll miss her from the class, but we'll look forward to her letters back to us. And of course we'll look forward to welcoming her when she has her next furlough.

"We promise to pray for you," Bob continued, turning to face Eileen. "Now let's pray, committing her to the Lord's care and a fruitful ministry."

There's a power beyond the power of any storm, or any nation, or Satan himself. "All power is given unto me," Jesus said. "Go and teach."

Eileen will be going in that power to teach in Singapore . . . an extension of our class.

August 20

I guess I'm not different from most other teachers in wanting to see immediate results, sudden changes in the people I teach.

Yet this seldom happens, and I must admit that my own life is an example of the time it takes to change, or be changed.

I find some comfort in the fact that when St. Paul said, "I have learned, in whatsoever state I am, therewith to be content" (Philippians 4:11), he was an old man. How long did it take the great apostle to learn the lesson of contentment in adverse circumstances, I wonder.

My responsibility is to teach God's Word; His is to change people. I have to learn to teach by faith—just as I'm to do everything else in my life by faith—rather than by sight. I must trust God for results, for change. I must believe that His Word will not return to Him void; it will accomplish His purpose.

The accomplishing may take years. Meanwhile, I planted a bomb in people's lives this morning, a delayed-action bomb that will go off at some future date. My responsibility is to plant the bomb. God's responsibility is to detonate it.

I hope I'm around to see it go off.